Hawai'i's Favorite
BENTO BOX
Recipes

Lots of Fun Lunches for Kids

Susan Yuen

Mutual Publishing

Library of Congress PCN available upon request.

ISBN-10: 1-56647-976-2
ISBN-13: 978-1-56647-976-9

First Printing, May 2013

Mutual Publishing, LLC
1215 Center Street, Suite 210
Honolulu, Hawai'i 96816
Ph: 808-732-1709 / Fax: 808-734-4094
email: info@mutualpublishing.com
www.mutualpublishing.com

Printed in Korea

Table of Contents

Part II—Recipes

Foreword

Four years have passed since the publication of my first cookbook, *Hawaiʻi's Bento Box Cookbook*. During that period of time, God blessed me with so many wonderful opportunities to meet other bento enthusiasts, share new bento ideas on my blog, create more diverse bentos for a second book, *Hawaiʻi's Bento Box Cookbook: Second Course*, and most importantly, create more bentos for my children, Paige and Sean.

Hawaiʻi's Favorite Bento Box Recipes is a compilation of my favorite bentos and recipes from my first two cookbooks. Following are the most creatively designed bentos from those books that are also quick and easy to make, even for the busiest mom. Included is a chapter on sandwiches which require no cooking time at all and feature lovable bears, birds, and baby chicks—sure to entice even your pickiest lunchtime eater. There are local favorites: a variety of musubi constructions, manapua, and fried rice, as well as dishes such as Korean Barbequed Beef, Miso-Teriyaki Chicken, and Shrimp Karaage that allow you to not only create attractive bentos, but dinner for the entire family.

These are my children's favorite family recipes because they are the reason I began this bento adventure. My goal was to show my kids how much joy and love they brought into my life. They continue to inspire me to make bentos, and I love seeing their excited expressions and lovable grins when they unpack their bento lunches.

I sincerely hope you have a great time recreating some of these fun and fanciful bentos for your child like I have. Mahalo to all of you for your continued support and enthusiasm for Hawaiʻi's Bento Box cookbooks!

Acknowledgments

I wish to thank God first and foremost, for all of the many blessings that He continually bestows upon me especially with family, friends, and our wonderful church.

I also want to thank my husband, best friend and love of my life, Mark, for all of his support, encouragement, crazy antics, and especially, his unconditional love.

 To my mom, Geraldine, thank you so much for taking so much of your time to baby-sit so that I could complete this book. Thank you also to Burt, Amy, Caitlin, and Dillon for all of your support, generosity, and love. To Mom and Dad Yuen and Burt and Mary Ann, thank you so much for your love, enthusiasm, advice, and support to Mark and me.

Thank you as well to the rest of our 'Ohana for I am extremely blessed to be surrounded by such loving relatives and friends.

I especially want to thank the Tsangs, Higas, and the Lees for being such an amazing source of friendship and love. You will always be family to us.

A special and heartfelt thank you to Kevin Fujitani, who took the time to contribute some of his amazing pictures to this book. I am honored and blessed to have worked with you!

Finally, I want to thank Paige and Sean for the joy that they bring to me everyday. I am forever grateful to our Lord, for He has blessed my life with you both and taught me so much in and through you. I love you both with all of my heart and soul.

Important Tips

DECORATIONS AND TOOLS

* Regarding the use of picks and decorations, **never use with younger children as it could pose a choking hazard.**

* Color Mist™ is food coloring in an aerosol spray form and is made by Wilton. It can be found at Compleat Kitchen, The Executive Chef, and online at Amazon.com.

* For round cutters, look around to see what you have. For smaller circles, use straws or pastry bag tips. In craft or kitchen stores they sell fondant cutters of various sizes. Also look for round cutter sets.

SECURING FOOD

* Very small pieces (¼-inch) of uncooked angel hair pasta and somen can be used to secure certain moist foods as indicated in the recipes. The pasta or somen does become soft after 2 hours. **Do not use if your child will eat it right away.**

* Peanut butter, jelly, icing, or mayonnaise may be used to secure foods as well.

PACKING FOOD

* Choose the right sized container and fill the container such that the food doesn't shift around during travel.

* To prevent sweating make sure that all of the cooked food is cooled to room temperature before packing.

* For hot thermal containers, spend the money on a good reputable one. Preheat the thermal container with hot water and ensure the food is hot when putting it into the thermal container.

* For cold lunches, pack with an ice pack or a frozen drink in an insulated bag.

part i
bentos

keiki cutouts

Ballerina
with Chicken Katsu and Tamago

1 slice bologna
1 slice cheddar cheese
5 slices kamaboko
Nori for mouth and eyes
Cake decorations *(silver dragées and flower decorations)*
Chicken Katsu *(see page 93)*
Tamago *(see page 117)*

1. With the bologna, use the circle cutter to cut out the girl's body. Then use the rabbit cutter to cut out the girl's head. Rotate the rabbit cutter 180 degrees to cut off the rabbit ears. Use one of the ears to make the girl's feet by cutting it in half.

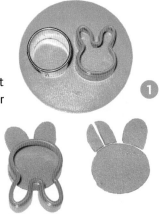

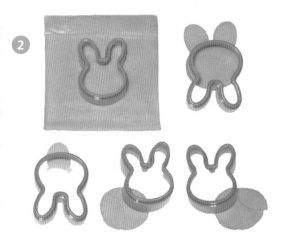

2. With the cheddar cheese, use the rabbit cutter to cut out the rabbit shape. Rotate the rabbit cutter 180 degrees to cut off the rabbit ears. Use the bottom edge of the rabbit cutter to cut out the bangs of the girl's hair. Cut off ½ of the rabbit's ear from the bottom. Use the top part of the ear for the girl's bun.

3. With the kamaboko, use the teardrop-shaped cutter to cut out 5 teardrops. Cut off 2 of the pointed top part of the teardrops about ⅓ of the way down to use as the top part of the dress. It will look like triangles.

With nori, punch out mouth and eyes.

4. Place the bologna head, the body of the girl, and her feet on a flat bed of rice. Use the cheese cutouts for the girl's bangs and the small cut rabbit ear as the bun for her hair. Place the 3 teardrop-shaped kamaboko about ⅓ of the way down her body to form her skirt. Then place the 2 triangular kamaboko cutouts above the skirt to form the top of her dress. Add eyes and a mouth. Then add the silver dragées to form the trim of her dress and hairpiece, and use the blue flowers to decorate the dress.

1 slice bologna
1 slice cheddar cheese
5 slices kamaboko
1 teaspoon green hana ebi *(Japanese colored shrimp flakes)*
Nori for mouth and eyes
Cake decorations for earrings and flower
Chicken Long Rice *(see page 90)*
Slow Cooker Kālua Pork *(see page 83)*

1. With the bologna, use the circle cutter to cut out the girl's body. Then use the rabbit cutter to cut out the girl's head. Rotate the rabbit cutter 180 degrees to cut off the rabbit ears. Use one of the ears to make the girl's feet by cutting it in half.

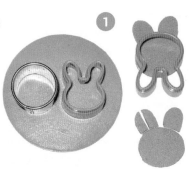

2. With the cheddar cheese, use the rabbit cutter to cut out the rabbit shape. Rotate the rabbit cutter 180 degrees to cut off the rabbit ears. Use the bottom edge of the rabbit cutter to cut out the bangs of the girl's hair. Also cut out a top for the girl using the "figure eight" shape cutter.

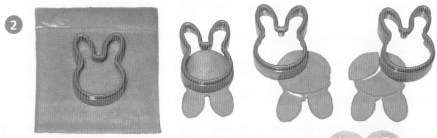

3. With the kamaboko, cut out three long teardrops to make the hula skirt. Also cut out one small flower for the girl's hair.

With nori, punch out a mouth and eyes.

4. Place the bologna head and the body of the girl on a flat bed of rice. Use the cheese cutouts for the girl's bangs and the rabbit ears as the girl's pigtails. Press the long teardrop-shaped kamaboko into the green ebi and place on the girl's body to form a skirt. Place the "figure eight" cheese top over the top of the skirt. Add bologna feet, eyes, and mouth, and the kamaboko flower for her hair. Add cake decorations to finish her flower and for her earrings.

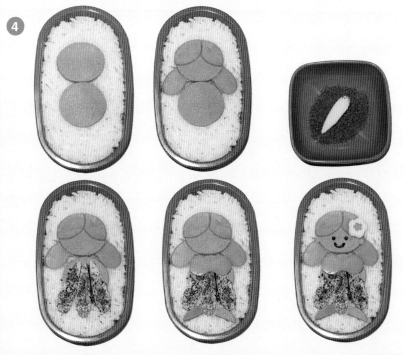

Surfer Boy
with Chap Chae and Barbeque Beef

Rice
1 slice bologna
1 slice cheddar cheese
1 cooked hotdog
Nori for eyes and mouth
Cake decorations for shorts
Chap Chae *(see page 113)*
Barbeque Beef *(see page 79)*

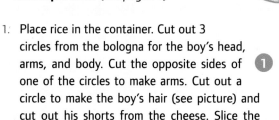

1. Place rice in the container. Cut out 3 circles from the bologna for the boy's head, arms, and body. Cut the opposite sides of one of the circles to make arms. Cut out a circle to make the boy's hair (see picture) and cut out his shorts from the cheese. Slice the hotdog on the bias to make a surfboard.

2. To assemble the boy, arrange the bologna head, body, arms, and feet. Add the boy's cheese hair and shorts, and his hotdog surfboard. Then cut his eyes and mouth out of the nori and place on his face. Add cake decorations to his shorts to complete.

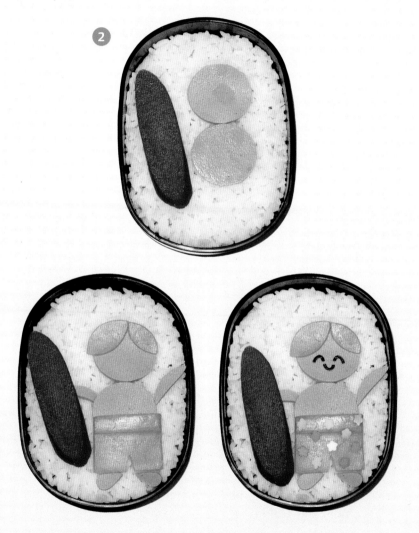

flying friends

Butterfly Soba
with Pan-seared Butter Kabocha

3 ounces cooked soba
¼ cup soba sauce *(store-bought)*, **kept in a separate container**
2 slices kamaboko
2 decorative picks
1 tablespoon sliced green onions
3 slice fish sausage or bologna
Pan-Seared Butter Kabocha
   (see page 111)

1. Place soba in the container and store sauce separately on the side.

2. Cut two butterflies from the kamaboko with a butterfly shaped cutter. Cut out four small circles from the pink part of the kamaboko for the butterfly's wings.

3. Stick the picks through where the butterfly's head would be, or you can cut two small hearts from the fish sausage in place of the picks (see photo). Place green onions on the soba in a small pile where the flowers would go.

4. Using a small flower shaped cutter, cut out three flowers and punch out the center with a small circle cutter.

Owl SPAM® Musubi
with Fish Cake Tamago

Rice
1 (¼-inch) slice of SPAM®
Nori
2 slices kamaboko
1 slice bologna
Fish Cake Tamago *(see page 117)*

Using a nigiri sushi mold, make 3 musubis. Cut SPAM® to fit the rice and pan-fry until cooked. Place the SPAM® on the rice. Wrap the SPAM® musubi with small strips of nori. Cut 6 eyes out of the kamaboko and 3 beaks out of the pink part of the kamaboko and arrange on the musubi. Cut 6 smaller circles out of the bologna for the inner part of the owl's eyes. Place bologna circles on the owl and finish with eyes punched out of nori.

Butterflies
with Matcha Green Tea Salmon Soba

1 slice cheddar cheese
1 slice mozzarella cheese
Nori for eyes and mouths
Matcha Green Tea Salmon
Soba *(see page 98)*

1. From the cheddar cheese cut out two butterflies and punch out four circles in each butterfly in the wing area.

2. From the mozzarella cut out four small ovals for the butterflies head and body to fit the butterflies (see picture).

3. Finish with nori eyes and mouths.

2

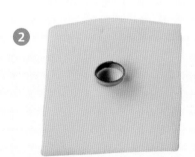

Blackbirds
with Teriyaki Chicken

Rice
2 jumbo pitted olives
2 carrot slices, blanched
2 slices kamaboko
Nori for stars and eyes
Teriyaki Chicken *(see page 94)*

Place rice in the container. Slice 2 olives in half. Use 3 of the halves as the blackbird bodies and arrange on the rice. Thinly slice the other half to make 2 wings for each bird. From the carrot, cut out 3 small triangle beaks for the birds and 6 V-shaped feet. Arrange on the birds. Cut out small circle eyes from the kamaboko and place them on the birds. Finish the eyes with small nori circles, and punch out stars to decorate the rice.

furry friends

Bear
Garlic Chicken Fried Rice

Garlic Chicken Fried Rice *(see page 92)*
4 slices kamaboko
Nori for eyes and nose

Place fried rice in an animal-shaped bowl. Out of the kamaboko, cut 2 large circles for the eyes, 1 small oval for the nose, and a crescent shape for the mouth. Place the kamaboko shapes on the fried rice. Cut eyes and a nose out of the nori to finish.

Rice
2 (¼-inch) slices of SPAM®
Teriyaki Sauce *(see page 94 or use store-bought)*
Nori
Chikuwa Hotdogs *(see page 120)*

With bunny- and bear-shaped rice molds or cookie cutters, form musubis. Use the mold or cutter to cut the bunny and bear shapes out of the SPAM®. Cook the SPAM® in the Teriyaki Sauce and place on the musubis. Wrap with small strips of nori.

Croquette Dog
with Teriyaki Hamburgers

Rice
1 croquette (store-bought)
2 olives
1 slice kamaboko
Nori for eyes
Carrot slices, blanched
Teriyaki Hamburgers (see page 76)

Place rice into the container. Cook the croquette as directed on the package, then place on the rice. Cut 2 olives in half and use 3 of the halves as the dog's ears and nose. Cut 2 circles out of the kamaboko for the eyes, and finish with 2 small circles punched out from the nori. Arrange the olives and eyes on the croquette. From the carrots, cut out 2 flowers and arrange on the rice.

Croquette Lion
with Chicken Yakisoba and Shoyu Hotdog

Chicken Yakisoba *(see page 91)*
1 croquette *(store-bought)*
2 olives
1 slice kamaboko
Nori
Rice
Shoyu Hotdog *(see page 80)*

Place yakisoba into the container. Cook the croquette as directed on the package. Place the croquette on the noodles. Cut 2 olives in half and use 3 of the halves as the lion's ears and nose. Cut 2 circles from the kamaboko for the eyes, then punch out eyes from the nori to finish the eyes. Arrange the eyes, ears, and nose on the lion.

To make the happy-face musubi, form a musubi out of rice. Take a strip of nori and punch a happy face on the nori using the nori punch. Wrap nori around musubi.

Sheep
with Tonkatsu

Rice
1 olive
1 slice kamaboko
Nori for eyes
Tonkatsu *(see page 84)*

Form the rice into an oblong musubi (or use rice mold). Slice the olive in half and place one half on the musubi for the head. With the other half of the olive, make 3 thin lengthwise slices for the ears and tail, and arrange on the sheep. Cut eyes from the kamaboko and finish with small circles punched out from the nori. Cover the top of the sheep's head and ears with a little rice.

Hotdog Sushi Bear

Sushi Rice *(recipe follows)*
2 cooked hotdogs
Nori

Fill a sushi mold half-way with rice, and place the hotdog in the center (see picture). Top off with more rice, then press down with the top part of the mold. Un-mold the sushi roll and wrap with a sheet of nori. Cut the sushi roll into 8 slices. From the leftover hotdog, cut thin slices for the bears' ears. Decorate each sushi slice with the hotdog ears and noses, and nori eyes and noses.

Sushi Rice for Kids
Makes 2 rolls

2 cups rice *(makes 4 cups cooked)*
2 tablespoons Japanese rice vinegar
2 tablespoons sugar
1 teaspoon salt

Wash rice until water runs clear, and cook with 2 cups of water. Combine the vinegar, sugar, and salt in a small bowl and mix well. When rice is done let steam for 15 minutes longer. Next, fold the vinegar mixture into the rice, and let cool before making sushi. Cover with a damp towel so that the rice doesn't become dry.

Kitty Musubi
with Sesame Chicken

Rice
2 slices fish sausage *(or 1 slice bologna)*
Nori
Black sesame seeds
Sesame Chicken *(see page 89)*

To make the cat, use a cat or bear shaped musubi mold for the rice. From the fish sausage, cut out a flower, a triangle for the ear, and a small oval for the nose. Then from the nori cut out three crescent shapes for the eyes and mouth, one small triangle for the ear, one medium triangle for the top of the head, and four small strips for the whiskers. Decorate the flower with black sesame seeds.

Bear Musubis
with Grandma Geri's Nishime

Rice
Nori
3 slices fish sausage, or 1 slice bologna
4 decorative picks
Grandma Geri's Nishime *(see page 105)*

With a cylinder shaped musubi mold, form rice. Cut two strips of nori for the bear's clothes and wrap around the musubi. Cut two small ovals for the muzzles and four small circles for the buttons. Then from the nori, cut out the eyes and noses. Finish by adding the decorative picks for the bear's ears.

Hummus Bear

Sun-Dried Tomato Hummus *(see page 114)*
2 olives
1 slice mozzarella cheese
Nori for eyes

Fill silicone cupcake cup with the Sun-Dried Tomato Hummus. Cut two olives in half. Use two halves for the ears and one half for the nose. For the bear's eyes, cut out two circles from the mozzarella cheese and finish with circles cut from the nori.

Field Mouse
with Sesame Eggplant

Rice
Thinly, diagonally sliced green onions
Fried fish cake patty
2 slices fish sausage *(or 1 slice bologna)*
1 slice kamaboko
Nori for eye
Sesame Eggplant
   (see page 106)

1. Place cooled rice evenly in container. Then decorate the rice with the green onions so that it looks like tall grass.

2. With a mouse shaped cutter, cut out the fried fish cake and place on rice.

3. From the fish sausage, cut out one small circle for the nose and two small teardrop shapes for the ears. Then cut out a circle for the mouse's eye and finish with a nori circle.

Panda Musubi
with Chicken Tofu

Rice
Nori
1 slice fish sausage or bologna
1 slice kamaboko
Chicken Tofu (see page 96)

Use a bear shaped musubi mold to form the rice. From the nori, cut out two half circles for the ears, two ovals for around the bear's eyes, two small circles for the eyes, and a mouth. Place on panda except for the two small circles. Then cut out a small circle from the fish sausage for the nose. Then cut two small circles from the kamaboko for the eyes and then finish the eyes with the two small nori circles that were previously cut.

Panda
with Fried Furikake Tofu

Rice
2 thick slices kamaboko
Nori
Fried Furikake Tofu *(see page 115)*

Form rice into an oval shaped musubi and place in a cupcake cup. Cut two small circles from the kamaboko for the panda's ears and prop up on the sides of the musubi. From the nori, cut two small circles for the ears, two small ovals for the eyes, and a nose, and mouth. Arrange nori cutouts on musubi.

1 fried fish cake patty
1 slice bologna
1 slice cheddar cheese
Nori for eyes
Udon with Asparagus and Bacon *(see page 86)*

Cut a large oval from the fried fish cake patty for the puppy's head. Then from the bologna, cut two medium sized ovals for the ears and a small oval for the nose. From the cheddar cheese, cut out two small flowers for the puppy's ears then finish with two small nori circles for the eyes.

Reindeer Musubi
with Garlic Butter Shrimp and Mushrooms

1 slice SPAM®
Rice
1 ume
1 slice kamaboko
Nori for eyes and mouth
Garlic Butter Shrimp and Mushrooms *(see page 100)*

Cut SPAM® with a leaf-shaped cutter for the antlers and pan fry to cook. Form a egg-shaped musubi with the rice and place in a silicone cupcake cup. Place SPAM® antlers on the wider end of the musubi. Press ume into the smaller end of the musubi for the reindeer's nose. Cut a circle from the kamaboko for the eye. Then from the nori, cut out the eye and a small crescent shape for the mouth.

Mouse
with Nori Chicken Burgers

Rice
2 slices kamaboko
Nori for ears and eyes
1 slice bologna
Black sesame seeds for whiskers
Nori Chicken Burgers *(see page 95)*

Form rice into an oval shaped musubi and place into cupcake cup. Cut out two circles for the mouse's ears from the kamaboko. Cut out two circles from the nori, place on ears, and then tuck in between the cupcake cup and the musubi. Cut out two crescent shapes from the nori for the eyes. Cut out an oval from the bologna for the mouse's nose. Finish the mouse with black sesame seeds for the whiskers.

island life

Bento Boys
with Miso-Teriyaki Chicken

Rice
Nori
2 tablespoons katsuobushi
Miso-Teriyaki Chicken *(see page 88)*

Form rice with a cylinder shaped musubi mold. With clean fluted craft scissors, cut two strips of nori for the clothes and wrap around the musubi. Also cut eyes and mouths from the nori for the faces. Place katsuobushi in a small bowl and dip one end of the rice into the flakes to make the hair.

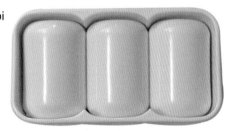

Coconut Tree
and Beef Stir-Fry with Black Bean Sauce

Rice
1 fried fish cake patty
Italian parsley
1 green onion
1 slice salami
1 slice kamaboko
Nori
Beef Stir-Fry with Black
    Bean Sauce *(see page 108)*

Place rice in the container. Cut out the coconut tree trunk
from the fried fish cake patty using a circle cutter then trim off
the ends with a knife. Arrange Italian parsley sprigs to look like palm
tree fronds. Add on a few slices of sliced green onions at the base of the
tree for the grass. Cut three circles from the salami for the coconuts. Then
cut six smaller circles from the kamaboko for the coconut's eyes. Finish
eyes with nori.

Flowers on Soba and Edamame
with Citrus Shoyu Dressing

2¼-inch slices of kamaboko
1¼-inch slice of fish sausage
3 decorative picks (optional)
Soba and Edamame with
Citrus Shoyu Dressing (see
page 116)

Cut flowers from kamaboko and fish sausage using a flower shaped cutter. Insert picks through the center of the flowers and place in soba. If you don't want to use the picks, you can just cut small circles from the pink part of the kamaboko for the flower centers (see photo).

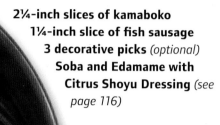

Flower Garlic Cheesy Bread
and Pasta with Meat Sauce

2 slices bread
2 tablespoons Garlic Butter, melted *(see page 121)*
1 tablespoon grated parmesan cheese
1 slice cheddar cheese
Pasta with Meat Sauce *(see page 77)*

Cut two flowers out of bread using a flower shaped cutter. Brush liberally with melted Garlic Butter and sprinkle evenly with grated parmesan cheese. Toast in toaster oven until golden; let cool. Cut two circles from the cheddar cheese and place them on the flowers.

Alternatively, you could use slices of a small baguette to make the garlic bread. Then use small fun shaped cutters to cut the cheddar cheese and place on the bread (see picture).

Keiki Bread
with Slow Cooker Roast Beef

2 slices of bread
1 slice cheddar cheese
1 slice bologna
Nori for eyes and
**   mouths**
1 slice fish sausage
Slow Cooker Roast Beef
    (see page 75)

1. Cut two slices of bread using a large circle cutter.

2. Using a fluted circle cutter, cut three fluted circles out of the cheddar cheese. Cut one of the fluted circles in half and place on the other two for the hair.

3. Then from the bologna, cut out two circles slightly smaller than fluted cutter. Cut the top part of the bologna circle off and place on the cheese.

4. Cut small eyes and mouths from the nori for the face.

5. Then from the fish sausage cut four small circles for the cheeks and a small flower for the girl's hair.

Little Girl Musubi

with Sautéed Shrimp with Sun-Dried Tomato and Parsley Butter

Rice
Nori
Black sesame seeds
1 slice of bologna
Sautéed Shrimp with
Sun-Dried Tomato
and Parsley Butter
(see page 103)

1. Form the rice into a triangle-shaped musubi.

2. Cut a narrow strip and bangs from the nori for the girl's hair (see photos).

3. Wrap with a piece of plastic wrap for a minute to help the nori stick to the rice.

4. Cut eyes, nose and mouth from the nori and arrange on the musubi.

5. Complete eyes with black sesame seeds for the eye lashes. From bologna cut 2 small circles and a flower to finish the little girl.

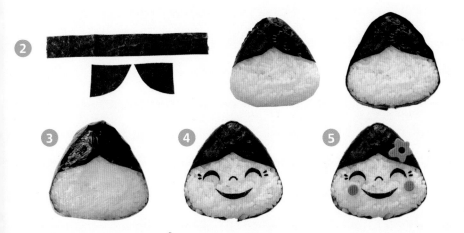

SPAM™ Flowers
with a Heart Shaped SPAM™ Tamago

SPAM™ Tamago *(see page 117)*
1 slice SPAM®
1 slice cheddar cheese
Nori for eyes and mouth

To make the heart with the SPAM™ tamago, cut one thick slice about two inches thick. Place the tamago slice with cut ends facing in an up and down direction, then slice the tamago in half from the top diagonally. Flip one of the halves over so that the wider ends meet and the pointed ends meet to form a heart.

To make the flowers, cut SPAM® with a flower shaped cutter. Fry SPAM® and cool. Cut out two cheddar cheese circles for the faces and place on cooled SPAM®. Finish with nori eyes and mouths.

Octopus and Fish Sushi
with Chinese Roast Pork Salad

2 slices SPAM®
1 hot dog
Rice
1 slice kamaboko
1 slice fish sausage, or 1
    slice bologna
Nori
Chinese Roast Pork Salad
    (see page 107)

1. Cut SPAM® with a fish-shaped cutter and then fry until cooked.

2. Cut hot dog in half and then slice lengthwise in half. Make two cuts halfway up the hot dog (on the cut end) so that it looks like tentacles, then boil in hot water or pan fry to cook.

3. Make three small rectangular musubis for the sushi and then place SPAM® and hot dog on it. Wrap thin strips of nori around the sushi.

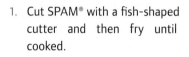

4. Cut four small circles for the eyes from the kamaboko.

5. Then cut two small ovals from the fish sausage (see photos) for the fins.

6. Finish with small nori circles for the eyes.

scrumptious sammies

1 slice bologna
1 slice cheddar
   cheese
Nori for eyes
Hoisin Mayo (recipe
   follows)
Chinese steamed bao
Chinese roast pork,
   thinly sliced
Thinly sliced green
   onions (optional)

Cut the ears, eyes, and nose out of
bologna. Then cut the insides of the eyes
and ears out of the cheese. With the nori punch,
cut out the eyes for the mouse.

To assemble, spread a little of the Hoisin Mayo on the inside of bun. Then add the
sliced roast pork and green onions. Place in the container then add the bologna
and cheese eyes, nose, and ears. Finish the eyes with the nori punchouts.

Hoisin Mayo

¼ cup mayonnaise
2 teaspoons hoisin sauce
¼ teaspoon sesame oil

Combine all ingredients and mix well.

Child's Name Sandwich

2 slices bread
Your favorite sandwich filling
1 slice cheddar cheese for name

Cut out bread with your choice of cutter.

Cut your child's name out of the cheddar cheese using the alphabet cutters. If your child has more letters than the space provided, either use his/her nickname or use a larger cutter for the sandwich.

Assemble the sandwich and place the child's name across it.

Char Siu Bunny Bao

1 slice bologna
1 slice cheddar cheese
Nori for eyes
2 slices of apple for ears
Hoisin Mayo *(see page 39)*
Chinese steamed bao
Char siu, thinly sliced
Green onion brush for hair
Thinly sliced green onions *(optional)*

Cut the eyes out of bologna. Then cut the inside of the ears and the nose out of the cheese. With a scissors cut out two circles for the eyes and use the nori punch to punch out a hole in each circle.

To assemble, spread a little of the Hoisin Mayo on the inside of bun. Then add in sliced char siu and green onions. Place in container then add on the bologna and cheese eyes and nose. Finish the eyes with the nori eyes. Place the apples slightly in the bun for the ears and complete with the cheese cutout for the inner ears. Cut a 2-inch piece from the bottom white part of the green onion. Thinly slice the top half of the cut piece until it looks like the picture. Insert green onion brush between the ears.

Acorn Girl Sandwich

2 slices of your favorite bread
Your favorite deli meat or sandwich filling
1 slice mozzarella cheese
1 slice bologna
1 slice cheddar cheese
Nori and black sesame seeds for eyes

1. Cut the two slices of bread using an acorn shaped cutter. Assemble sandwich with your favorite deli meat or sandwich filling.

2. Cut the mozzarella with the same acorn shape and place on bread.

3. Then cut the bologna with the same cutter for the hair (see photos).

4. Next cut the cheddar cheese with the acorn cutter and a large circle cutter to make the hat (see photos).

5. Also cut a small flower from the cheddar cheese for the hat and a small crescent shape for the mouth.

6. Cut out eyes from the nori and finish with black sesame seeds for the lashes.

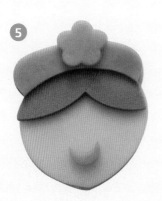

Bear SPAM™, Egg, and Cheese
Breakfast Sandwich

1 roll
1 egg scrambled
1 slice of SPAM®
1 slice cheddar cheese
Nori for the eyes and nose

Take a roll and fill evenly with scrambled eggs. Take a small bear cutter and cut two bear shapes from the SPAM®. Fry SPAM® and place the torso of the bears into the sandwich. Cut two small ovals from the cheddar cheese to use as the bear's muzzles and place on SPAM®. Tuck the rest of the cheese in the sandwich. Finish the bear with the nori eyes and noses.

Birdie Sandwich
with Clam Chowder

2 slices of bread
Your favorite deli meat or sandwich filling
1 slice cheddar cheese
2 slices fish sausage or 1 slice bologna
1 slice mozzarella cheese
Nori for eye
Clam Chowder *(see page 97)*

Cut two circles from the bread and assemble sandwich with your favorite deli meat or sandwich filling. Using a bird-shaped cutter, cut a bird from the cheddar cheese. From the fish sausage cut a teardrop shape for the wing and a small triangle for the beak. Cut a circle from the mozzarella for the eye and finish with a circle cut from the nori.

2 slices of brown bread
Your favorite deli meat or sandwich filling
1 slice of mozzarella cheese
1 slice bologna
2 small sugar eyes
Icing or peanut butter for "glue" *(optional)*

Cut out the bread using a bear-shaped cutter. Assemble the sandwich with your favorite filling. From the mozzarella cheese, cut out an oval for the bear's muzzle and two small circles for the buttons. Cut out a small circle for the nose and a bowtie from the bologna. Fasten the cutouts and sugar eyes with icing or peanut butter (optional).

Chick Sandwiches

1 roll
Your favorite deli meat
   or sandwich filling
1 slice cheddar cheese
1 slice bologna
Nori for eyes

1. Assemble the sandwich with your favorite filling and slice in half. Place sandwich in the container, side by side.

2. With a fluted circle cutter, cut out the chicks from the cheddar cheese. Using an oval-shaped cutter cut the wings for the chicks from the cheese as well.

3. Cut out two circles from the bologna and then cut the circles in half for their beaks. Finish with nori eyes.

Angel Fish Sandwich

2 slices of your favorite bread
Your favorite deli meat of
   sandwich filling
1 slice cheddar cheese
Fish sausage *(or other type of pink*
   meat like ham or the pink part of
   kamaboko)
1 slice kamaboko
Nori for then eye

1. Cut out the bread and deli meat with a circle shaped cutter, then assemble sandwich.

2. Cut out the cheddar cheese with an angel fish-shaped cutter and trim the fish with the circle cutter so that it fits the bread.

3. Cut a heart out of the cheddar cheese and place on the fish for the fin. Cut out small circles from the fish sausage and place along the fish's back and a small heart for the mouth.

4. With a larger circle cut an eye out of the kamaboko and finish it with nori.

Aloha Pig Sandwich
and Portuguese Bean Soup with Fun Pasta

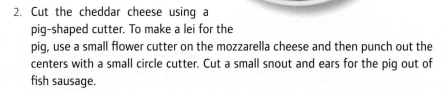

2 slices of bread
Your favorite
  deli meat
  or sandwich
  filling
1 slice cheddar
  cheese
1 slice mozzarella
  cheese
1 slice fish
  sausage or
  bologna
Nori and black sesame
  seeds for the eyes
Portuguese Bean Soup
  with Fun Pasta *(see
  page 81)*

1. Cut two circles from the bread. Assemble sandwich with your favorite sandwich filling.

2. Cut the cheddar cheese using a pig-shaped cutter. To make a lei for the pig, use a small flower cutter on the mozzarella cheese and then punch out the centers with a small circle cutter. Cut a small snout and ears for the pig out of fish sausage.

3. Finish pig with a nori eye and black sesame seeds for the lashes.

Frog Sandwich

2 slices of your favorite bread
Your favorite deli meat or sandwich filling
1 slice cheddar cheese
2 large sugar eyes
Icing or peanut butter for "glue"

Cut bread using a frog-shaped cutter. Assemble sandwich with your choice of filling. Using an oval-shaped cutter, cut out two ovals from the cheddar cheese. Place one of the ovals on the frog's stomach and then cut a crescent shape from the other oval to make the frog's mouth. Cut out two small circles for the frog's nose. Fasten the cheese cutouts and the eyes to the bread with a small amount of icing or peanut butter.

Kitty SPAM™ Sandwich

2 slices SPAM®
1 roll
1 leaf of lettuce
1 slice cheddar
  cheese
1 slice
  mozzarella
  cheese
2 pieces
  uncooked
  somen noodles
  *(optional—somen
  needs to be removed before
  eating)*
Nori for eyes

1. With an oval shaped cutter, cut two ears for the cat out of the SPAM®. Fry SPAM® and let cool.

2. Take a roll and fill with lettuce.

3. From the cheddar and mozzarella cheese cut out 2 hearts from each cheese and arrange in sandwich. Add cooled SPAM®.

4. Then cut out two circles from the mozzarella cheese for the eyes and oval and crescent shape for the nose and mouth. Then take the somen and stick small pieces in the cat for the whiskers (optional for older kids and should be omitted entirely for younger children). The somen will need to be removed before eating as it will still be hard. Finish the eyes with circles cut from nori.

Polar Bear Sandwich

2 slices white bread
Your favorite deli meat or sandwich filling
1 slice cheddar cheese
1 slice salami
1 sugar eye

Cut the two slices of bread using a polar bear-shaped cutter. Assemble the sandwich with your favorite deli meat or sandwich filling. From the cheddar cheese, cut out a medium-sized circle for the polar bear's tail, a small circle for his nose, and a crescent shape for his mouth. Cut out small circles that range in size for the bear's spots from the salami. Finish bear with a sugar eye.

Pumpkin Sandwich

2 slices of your favorite bread
Your favorite deli meat or sandwich filling
1 slice cheddar cheese
1 slice bologna
2 sugar eyes

Cut out two pieces of bread using a pumpkin-shaped cutter. Fill with your favorite sandwich filling. Using the same pumpkin shaped cutter cut out cheddar cheese and place on bread. Cut also a crescent shape for the mouth. Cut the bologna with the pumpkin cutter, then use the bottom of the cutter to cut the top off to use as the pumpkin stem. Finish with sugar eyes.

T-Rex PBJ Sandwiches

4 slices of your favorite bread
Peanut Butter
Jelly
2 large sugar eyes
White icing *(optional)*
Cheddar cheese

Cut out the bread with a dinosaur shaped cutter. Assemble sandwich with the peanut butter and jelly. Attach sugar eyes to sandwich with a small dab of peanut butter (or icing) on the backs of each eye. Cut small stars out of the cheddar cheese and attach to dinosaur with a small amount of peanut butter or icing.

Teddy Bear Sandwich

2 slices of bread
Your favorite deli meat or sandwich filling
1 slice bologna
1 slice mozzarella cheese
1 slice cheddar cheese
Nori for eyes

1. Cut out two large circles for the bear's head and two small circles for the ears from the bread. Assemble the sandwich with the two larger pieces of bread and your favorite sandwich filling.

2. Place the sandwich in your container and prop the two smaller bread circles on the side for the ears.

3. From the bologna, cut out two circles for the ears and one oval for the nose.

4. Using the mozzarella cheese cut out two small circles for the eyes and then from the cheddar cheese cut a crescent shape for the mouth.

5. Finish eyes with small circles cut from nori.

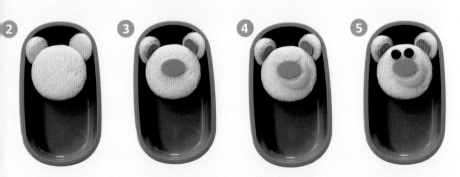

Yellow Bird Sandwich

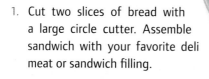

2 slices bread
Your favorite deli meat or
sandwich filling
1 slice cheddar cheese
1 slice bologna
1 slice mozzarella
Nori and black sesame
seeds for eyes

1. Cut two slices of bread with a large circle cutter. Assemble sandwich with your favorite deli meat or sandwich filling.

2. Cut a circle from the cheddar cheese using the same circle cutter and place on sandwich.

3. Using a medium sized circle cutter, cut out two leaf shaped pieces from bologna for the beak (see photos) and place on the sandwich.

4. Cut two circles for the eyes using a small circle cutter from the mozzarella cheese.

5. Then using a fluted circle cutter, cut the feathers for the top of the birds head. from the mozzarella as well.

6. Finish eyes with nori and black sesame seeds for the lashes.

rice 'n more

Gecko
with Mochiko Chicken and Tamago

Rice
1 egg, beaten
3 carrot slices, blanched
1 slice kamaboko
Nori for eyes
Soybean
Black sesame seeds for bug's eyes

Place rice into the container. Cook the beaten egg in a nonstick pan on low heat. Flip the omelet once and cool.

1. Cut the omelet with a gecko-shaped cutter, then place the gecko on the rice.

2. With the carrot, cut out 2 small heart-shaped wings for the bug and several small circles for the gecko's spots. Arrange the spots on gecko and place the wings on the rice. Cut out 2 small circles from the kamaboko for the gecko's eyes.

3. Finish with eyes cut out from nori. Place the soybean on the carrot wings and finish the bug with the 2 black sesame seed eyes.

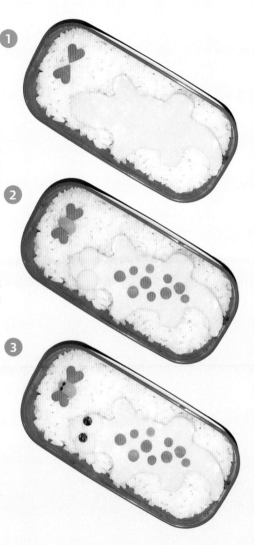

Teriyaki Meatball Worm
with Furikake Imitation Crab Noodles

Rice
Furikake
¼ pound of Teriyaki Hamburger recipe *(see page 76)*
2 tablespoons Teriyaki Sauce *(see page 94 or use store-bought)*
1 thin slice kamaboko
Nori for eye
2 carrot slices, blanched
Furikake Imitation Crab Noodles *(see page 104)*

Place rice in the container. Mix a little furikake with a small amount of rice for the ground. With wet fingers, place the furikake rice onto the white rice.

Roll the Teriyaki Hamburger into small meatballs and fry until just cooked. Drain the excess fat and add Teriyaki Sauce. Toss in the sauce and cook for a few seconds longer. Arrange the meatballs on the rice to look like a worm.

Cut out a small circle from the kamaboko for the eye. Then punch out a small circle from the nori and place on the kamaboko to finish the eye, and place on worm.

With the carrots, cut out small flowers and decorate the rice.

Dinosaur
with Teriyaki Steak

Rice
1 egg, beaten
Carrot slices, blanched
Nori for eye
Teriyaki Steak *(see page 78)*

Place rice into the container. Cook the beaten egg in a non-stick pan on low heat. Flip the omelet once and cool. Cut the omelet with a dinosaur-shaped cutter, then place the dinosaur on the rice. From the carrot, cut out 1 star to decorate the rice and several small circles for the dinosaur's body. Arrange carrot spots on the dinosaur and cut the rest of the circles in half and place on the ridge of his back. Finish the dinosaur with an eye cut from nori.

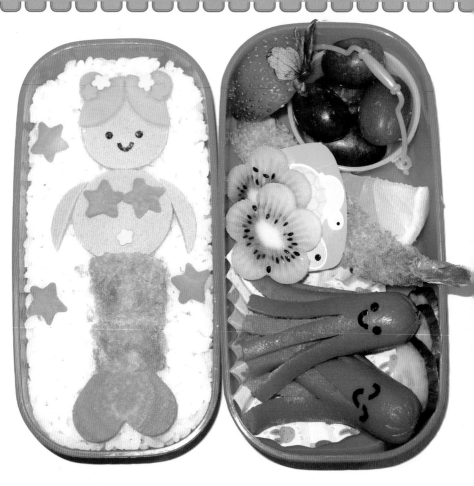

Rice
1 slice bologna
1 slice cheddar cheese
3 carrot slices, blanched
Fried Shrimp *(see page 101)*
Nori for eyes and mouth
Cake decorations
1 hotdog

1. Place rice in the container. With a bear-shaped cutter, cut the head for the mermaid from the bologna. Then cut out 2 circles, 1 for the body, and cut the sides of the other circle to make arms.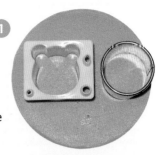

2. Using the bear cutter again, cut the hair out of the cheese (see picture).

 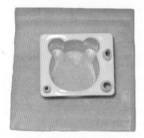  

Cut 5 small stars and 1 heart out of the carrot. Cut the pointed end of the heart off; the rest of the heart will be used for the mermaid's tail fin.

3. Arrange the mermaid's head, hair, body, and arms on the rice. Cut the tail off the Fried Shrimp and use it as the mermaid's tail with the carrot heart as the fins. Use the carrot stars for the mermaid's top and decorate the rice with the rest of the stars. Add her nori eyes and mouth and finish her hair and belly button with the cake decorations.

To make the hotdog octopus, cut a hotdog in half and make slits (about $^2/_3$ the length of the hotdog) from the cut end to make tentacles. Cook in boiling water until heated through and the tentacles separate. When cool, add the nori eyes and mouth.

Octopus
with Bacon and Portuguese Sausage Fried Rice

Bacon and Portuguese Sausage Fried Rice *(see page 85)*
1 egg, beaten
3 carrot slices, blanched
1 slice kamaboko
Nori for eyes and mouth

Place fried rice into the container. Cook the beaten egg in a nonstick pan on low heat. Flip the omelet once and cool. Cut the omelet with an octopus-shaped cutter, then place the octopus on the fried rice. From the carrot, cut out several small circles for the octopus's tentacles and 2 star shapes. Place the starfishs on the rice and arrange the carrot circles on the tentacles. Cut out 2 small circles for the eyes, and a crescent shape for the mouth from the kamaboko and arrange on the octopus. Cut out the octopus's eyes and the starfishs' eyes and mouths from the nori.

Penguin SPAM® Musubi
with Macaroni Salad

Rice
1 (¼-inch) slice SPAM®
Nori
3 slices kamaboko
Macaroni Salad *(see page 110)*

Using a nigiri sushi mold, make 3 musubis. Cut SPAM® to fit the rice and pan-fry until cooked. Place the SPAM® on the rice. Cut 3 sheets of nori to fit the SPAM® musubi and wrap with the nori. Cut 6 small circles out of the kamaboko for the eyes and 6 larger half-circles for the wings. From the pink part of the kamaboko, cut 3 small tri-angles for the beaks. Arrange the eyes, wings, and beaks on the penguins. Finish the penguins with eyes punched out from the nori.

Mini Portuguese Sausage Frittata
with Bear Bread and Guava Butter

1 slice bread
Mini Portuguese Sausage Frittata *(see page 87)*
Guava Butter *(see page 123)*

Cut out the bread with a bear-shaped cutter and pack in bento along with the Portuguese Sausage Frittata and a small container of Guava Butter.

Mini Manapua Bento

Makes 50 mini manapua

5 cans buttermilk biscuit dough *(7.5 ounce wt)*
Manapua filling *(see page 119)*
1 egg beaten
Red food coloring and a clean small stamp *(optional)*

1. Pre-heat oven to 400 degrees.

2. Prepare a cookie sheet with parchment paper or silpat. Dust your work space with flour, and your hands with flour to prevent dough from sticking.

3. There are 10 biscuits per container. Flatten a biscuit into a circle and place a heaping teaspoon of filling on the biscuit and pull sides together and crimp to form a ball.

4. Place crimped side down on the pan.

5. Right before baking, lightly brush top with egg wash and let dry for a minute.

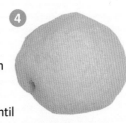

6. Put a drop of red food coloring on a plate and dip stamp in it, tapping off the excess.

7. Stamp the top of manapua and bake for 12 minutes or until tops are golden brown.

1 triangle shaped musubi
1 sheet nori
3 slices of fish sausage (or 1 slice bologna)
1 ume
Kabocha with Shiitake Mushrooms and Pork (see page 82)

Wrap the bottom half of the musubi with nori. Cut out three circles from the fish sausage: two for the wheels, and one cut in half and trimmed on the bottom for the cars windows. Place the ume on top of the car the slightly push into the rice to hold.

Pumpkin Musubis
with Korean BBQ Beef

Rice
Orange Color Mist™
3 slices fish sausage *(or 1 slice bologna)*
2 sprigs Italian parsley
Nori and black sesame seeds for the eyes
Korean Barbequed Beef *(see page 74)*

Form the rice into pumkin-shaped musubis. Spray with orange Color Mist™ and let dry for a minute. From the fish sausage cut 2 small ovals for the noses and a flower for the girl pumpkin. Place a parsley spring for the vine on top of each pumpkin and then place the flower on the girl pumpkin's vine. Cut small nori circles for the eyes and finish with black sesame seeds for the girl's lashes.

Stars and Hearts Snack Bento

Thick slices of mozzarella
Thick slice of ham *(or turkey)*
Crackers and fruit

Cut out three stars from the mozzarella using a star shaped cutter. Then cut out three hearts from the ham using a heart shaped cutter. Stack the cheese and ham cutouts in the bento box along with crackers and fruit.

Teddy Bear
Peel and Eat Cheese Snack

2 slices American cheese singles
2 slices Swiss cheese singles

Unwrap all of the American and Swiss cheese carefully. Stack on top of each other alternating the American cheese and the Swiss cheese. Cut out from the cheese four bears using a metal bear-shaped cookie cutter (plastic ones don't work as well).

Cold Udon *(see page 112)*
2 to 3 pieces of Shrimp Karaage *(see page 102)*
Fun umbrella pick

Fill a small Chinese takeout box with Cold Udon. Place 2 to 3 Shrimp Karaage on the top and top with a fun umbrella pick. Great for a keiki party!

part ii
recipes

beef

1 cup shoyu
½ cup apple juice
2 tablespoons sake
½ teaspoon sesame oil
1 cup sugar
3 cloves crushed garlic
½ teaspoon grated ginger
3 stalks of green onions cut into 1-inch pieces
1 teaspoon toasted sesame seeds
1½ pounds thinly sliced beef

Combine shoyu, apple juice, sake, sesame oil, sugar, garlic, ginger, green onions, and toasted sesame seeds. Reserve ¼ cup of sauce for basting. Marinate the beef in the rest of the sauce overnight. Broil or grill meat until done. When serving, slice and baste meat with sauce.

Slow Cooker Roast Beef
Serves 6

3 pounds boneless chuck roast
1 teaspoon salt
¼ teaspoon pepper
½ cup flour
4 tablespoons oil
2 envelopes onion
**   soup mix**
2 tablespoons tomato
**   paste**
3 cloves garlic, crushed
1 (14-ounce) can
**   chicken broth**
1½ cups water
½ cup water mixed with 4
**   tablespoons cornstarch**
1 tablespoon sugar

Cut the chuck roast into four equal
pieces. Season with salt and pepper,
then toss in flour until evenly coated. In
a frying pan on medium high heat, heat oil and
brown the pieces of chuck roast evenly on all sides. When done place roast in crock
pot and add in onion soup mix, tomato paste, garlic, chicken broth, and 1½ cups
of water. Cook in crock pot on high for about 5 hours (about 6 hours for smaller
ones) until meat is fork tender. When meat is done cooking, skim off all of the fat.
To make the gravy, mix the sauce with cornstarch and water mixture and sugar.
Cover and let thicken for a few minutes. Before serving, slice or shred meat and
serve with the gravy.

Teriyaki Hamburgers
Serves 6

2 pounds ground beef
2 eggs
3 stalks green onion, thinly sliced
½ cup bread crumbs
½ cup mayonnaise
1 teaspoon pepper
2 teaspoons onion powder
1 teaspoon salt
2 tablespoons or more Teriyaki Sauce for basting
   (see page 94 or use store-bought)

Combine all ingredients. Form into patties and cook until cooked through. Baste with Teriyaki Sauce.

Pasta with Meat Sauce

Serves 4

2 tablespoons olive oil
1 pound lean ground beef
¼ teaspoon salt
¼ teaspoon pepper
½ medium sized onion diced ¼-inch
2 cloves garlic, minced
1 (14.5-ounce) can sliced stewed tomatos
1 (1-pound 10-ounce) jar marinara sauce *(we like Prego®)*
1 pound dry pasta cooked

In a sauce pot heat olive oil. Then add beef, salt, and pepper, and cook until nicely browned. Add in the onion and garlic, and sauté until onion is soft. Then add in the stewed tomatoes. Break them into smaller (1- to 2-inch) pieces and cook for 2 to 3 minutes until most of the liquid has reduced down. Add in the marinara sauce, lower heat, and simmer for 15 to 20 minutes, stirring occasionally. Serve over cooked pasta.

Teriyaki Steak

Serves 4

1½ pounds steak
2¼ cups Teriyaki Sauce (*see page 94 or use store-bought*)
Green onions and sesame seeds to garnish

Marinate steak overnight in 2 cups Teriyaki Sauce. Grill or broil until desired doneness. Brush with the reserved ¼ cup Teriyaki Sauce. Slice to serve and garnish with green onions and sesame seeds.

BBQ Beef

Serves 4

1 cup shoyu
¼ cup mirin
½ cup sugar
½ cup red miso
2 tablespoons sesame oil
4 cloves garlic, minced
1 teaspoon ginger, grated
1 tablespoon toasted sesame seeds
2 tablespoons thinly sliced green onions
1½ pounds thinly sliced beef

Combine the shoyu, mirin, sugar, miso, sesame oil, garlic, ginger, sesame seeds, and green onions in a bowl and mix well. Reserve ¼ cup of marinade to brush on after cooking. Add beef and marinate for 20 to 30 minutes. Grill or pan-fry until done. Brush with extra sauce if desired.

Shoyu Hotdogs

Serves 4 as a side

4 hotdogs, sliced on the bias
¼ cup shoyu
¼ cup sugar

Add hotdogs, shoyu, and sugar to a small pot. Cook on medium until heated through.

Portuguese Bean Soup
with Fun Pasta
Serves 8

6 ounces bacon, sliced ¼-inch
12 ounces Portuguese sausage,
  sliced ¼-inch
1 large carrot, cut into
  ¼-inch pieces
2 large stalks of celery
  cut into ¼-inch pieces
1 medium onion, cut
  into ¼-inch pieces
2 cloves garlic minced
2 cups water
2 (14.5-ounce) cans beef
  broth
1 (49.5-ounce) can
  chicken broth
1 (14.5-ounce) can stewed
  tomatoes, sliced
1 (15-ounce) can kidney
  beans
1 bay leaf
1 teaspoon oregano
3 ounces of tomato paste
½ teaspoon pepper
2 cups of cabbage, chopped into ½-inch pieces
1 large russet potato, cut into ½-inch cubes
¼ cup parsley, chopped
3 ounces of dry pasta, cooked

In a large pot, cook bacon on medium high until almost crisp. Add in Portuguese sausage and cook for a few minutes. Then add in the carrots, celery, onion, and garlic; cook until soft (about 3 to 4 minutes). Add in the water, beef broth, chicken broth, tomatoes, kidney beans, bay leaf, oregano, tomato paste, pepper, and cabbage. Bring to a boil and then lower heat to medium and simmer for 25 minutes. Skim fat and then add in the potatoes. Cook for another 20 minutes, add in parsley and pasta.

Kabocha
with Shiitake Mushrooms and Pork
Serves 3

4 ounces ground or thinly sliced pork
¼ cup shoyu
¼ cup sugar
⅛ cup mirin
1 cup water
½ teaspoon dashi no moto
5 large fresh or rehydrated shiitake mushrooms sliced ¼-inch
1½ pounds of kabocha, cut into 1- to 1½-inch cubes

In a large sauce pot, combine pork, shoyu, sugar, mirin, water, and dashi no moto, and cook on medium high until pork is just cooked. Skim off the fat if there is any. Then add in kabocha and mushrooms, and bring to a boil. Lower heat to medium. Let simmer for about 15 minutes, stirring occasionally (and carefully so that the pumpkin doesn't break apart) until the pumpkin is cooked through. Be careful not to overcook, or pumpkin will get mushy.

Slow Cooker Kālua Pork

Serves 8 to 10

4- to 5-pound pork shoulder
2 tablespoons Liquid Smoke
2 tablespoons Hawaiian
  salt
2 large ti leaves
1 cup water

Rub pork all over with Liquid Smoke and Hawaiian salt, then wrap in 2 clean ti leaves. Place pork in slow cooker, add 1 cup of water to the bottom of the slow cooker and cover. Cook on high for 5 to 6 hours until the pork is easily shredded. When done, remove pork from slow cooker, discard ti leaves, and shred pork by hand or by using two forks. Sprinkle shredded pork with a little of the cooking liquid to season.

Tonkatsu
Serves 4

1½ pounds pork cutlet
Garlic salt and pepper to
taste
1 cup flour
3 eggs
1 tablespoon water
1 teaspoon sugar
3 cups panko
*(Japanese bread
crumbs)*
Oil for frying

Pat pork cutlets dry with a paper towel, then season with garlic salt and pepper. Lightly dredge pork in flour and shake off excess. Beat the 3 eggs with water and sugar to make an egg wash. Dredge floured pork in egg and finally in panko. Deep-fry in oil until golden and cooked through. Serve with Katsu Sauce (recipe follows).

Katsu Sauce

1 cup ketchup
1 tablespoon Worcestershire sauce
⅛ teaspoon pepper

Combine all ingredients and mix well.

Bacon and Portuguese Sausage Fried Rice

Serves 4

2 eggs, beaten
6 ounces bacon, cut into ¼-inch pieces
4 ounces Portuguese sausage, cut into ¼-inch pieces
6 cups day-old cooked rice
1½ tablespoons oyster sauce
¾ teaspoon garlic salt
¼ teaspoon pepper
½ cup frozen peas and
  carrots

Scramble beaten eggs and reserve. In a large pan, cook bacon until almost crisp then add Portuguese sausage and cook until browned. Add rice, oyster sauce, garlic salt, pepper, and peas and carrots. Mix until seasonings are evenly distributed throughout the rice. Remove from heat and fold in scrambled eggs.

Udon
with Asparagus and Bacon
Serves 3

8 ounces of bacon, sliced ¼-inch
1 pound asparagus (cut off woody ends) sliced ½-inch on the bias
2 tablespoons sake
½ cup chicken broth
12 ounces (dry weight) udon, cooked al dente
¼ teaspoon of pepper
½ teaspoon of salt
2 tablespoons Garlic Butter *(see page 121)*
Small lemon wedge

In a pan on medium-high heat, fry bacon until crisp. Drain most of the fat. Add in asparagus and stir-fry for about 15 seconds. Add in the sake and stir-fry for another 15 seconds. Add in chicken broth, udon, pepper, salt, and Garlic Butter. Toss in pan until combined and noodles are heated through. Remove from heat and squeeze a small lemon wedge over the top, or serve lemon on the side.

Mini Portuguese Sausage Frittatas
Makes 8

About 1 cup of frozen shredded hash browns
4 ounces of Portuguese sausage cut into ¼-pieces*
3 tablespoons green onions, sliced
6 extra large eggs
½ teaspoon salt
¼ teaspoon pepper
2½ tablespoons cheddar cheese, shredded

Preheat the oven to 350 degrees. On a baking tray, fill eight silicone baking cupcake cups halfway with frozen shredded hash browns. Cook Portuguese sausage in a frying pan and then divide equally among the cups and add sliced green onions. Beat the 6 eggs well and season with salt and pepper. Divide equally into the cups and then top with the cheddar cheese. Bake for about 15 to 20 minutes until eggs are set, depending on your oven the time may vary slightly.

*You can also substitute with different fillings like bacon, SPAM®, ham, mushrooms, spinach, zucchini, and so much more. Just make sure that you cook the filling first before adding it in.

Miso-Teriyaki Chicken
Serves 6

½ cup red miso
¼ cup shoyu
½ cup sugar
2 tablespoons mirin
1 tablespoon garlic, minced
½ teaspoon ginger, grated
½ teaspoon salt
2½ pounds boneless, skinless chicken thighs

To make the marinade, combine the miso, shoyu, sugar, mirin, garlic, ginger, and salt; mix well. Toss chicken in the marinade and let sit for 2 to 8 hours. The longer you let the chicken marinate the stronger the miso flavor will be. Grill or broil until cooked through.

Sesame Chicken
Serves 5

4 tablespoons mochiko flour
4 tablespoons cornstarch
4 tablespoons sugar
2 eggs
2 tablespoons shoyu
2 tablespoons oyster sauce
2 teaspoons black sesame seeds
1½ pounds boneless, skinless chicken thighs, cut into bite-sized pieces

Combine the mochiko flour, cornstarch, sugar, eggs, shoyu, oyster sauce, and black sesame seeds in a large bowl; stir until mixed well. Add chicken and marinate overnight. Before frying, mix the chicken in the marinade well. Drop the chicken one at a time into hot oil and deep-fry until browned and cooked through.

Chicken Long Rice

Serves 4

2 (1.875-ounce) packages long rice
1 tablespoon oil
1 pound chicken thighs or breasts, cut into ¼-inch slices
1 clove garlic, minced
2 (14.5-ounce) cans chicken broth
1 small (thumb-sized) piece ginger, sliced
1 teaspoon Hawaiian salt
¼ teaspoon pepper
1 tablespoon sliced green onions

Cook long rice in boiling water for about 4 to 5 minutes, then drain and set aside. Heat oil in a pan and cook chicken and garlic until cooked through. Stir in chicken broth, ginger, salt, and pepper and long rice. Let simmer for 15 minutes on medium-low heat. Garnish with sliced green onions before serving.

Chicken Yakisoba
Serves 4

1 pound yakisoba noodles *(follow directions on package on how to prepare noodles for cooking)*

12 ounces boneless skinless chicken thighs or breasts, cut into ¼-inch slices

1 tablespoon shoyu

1 teaspoon mirin

½ teaspoon salt

¼ teaspoon pepper

1 small clove garlic, minced

1½ tablespoons oil

1 small carrot, julienned

1 cup bean sprouts

¼ cup kamaboko, julienned

3 tablespoons oyster sauce

½ teaspoon hondashi *(Japanese bonito fish soup base)*

¼ teaspoon pepper

3 stalks green onion, cut into 1-inch pieces

Prepare yakisoba for cooking by loosening noodles with your hands or by running them under hot water. In a bowl marinate cut chicken in a mixture of shoyu, mirin, salt, pepper, and garlic for about 10 minutes. In a hot large pan, add oil and chicken; cook until chicken is cooked through. Add carrots, yakisoba, bean sprouts, kamaboko, oyster sauce, hondashi, and pepper. Cook and mix until seasonings are well distributed and noodles are heated through. Toss in green onions and remove from heat.

Garlic Chicken Fried Rice

Serves 4

10 ounces chicken tenders, cut into ¼- to ½-inch pieces
2 cloves minced garlic
2 tablespoons shoyu
½ teaspoon pepper, divided
2 eggs, beaten
2 tablespoons oil
6 cups day-old cooked rice
1½ tablespoons oyster sauce
½ cup frozen peas and carrots
1 tablespoon chopped chives

Marinate chicken in garlic, shoyu, and ¼ teaspoon pepper for 15 minutes. In the meantime, scramble beaten eggs and reserve. Add oil to a large pan and cook marinated chicken on medium-high heat until cooked through. Add rice, oyster sauce, and pepper. Mix to evenly distribute seasonings. Add peas and carrots and cook until fried rice is heated through. Remove from heat and fold in eggs and chopped chives.

Chicken Katsu
Serves 4

8 boneless skinless chicken thighs
Garlic salt and pepper to taste
1 cup flour
3 eggs
1 tablespoon water
1 teaspoon sugar
3 cups panko (*Japanese bread crumbs*)
Oil for frying

Pat chicken thighs dry with a paper towel, then season with garlic salt and pepper. Lightly dredge chicken in flour and shake off excess. Beat the 3 eggs with water and sugar to make an egg wash. Dredge floured chicken in egg and finally in panko. Deep-fry in oil until golden and cooked through. Serve with Katsu Sauce (see recipe on page 84).

Teriyaki Chicken
Serves 4

1 cup shoyu
¼ cup peanut butter
¾ cup sugar
3 cloves garlic, crushed
¼-inch thumb-sized slice ginger, crushed
3 stalks green onion, cut into 1-inch pieces
1½ pounds chicken thighs

Combine shoyu, peanut butter, sugar, garlic, and ginger in a sauce pot. Heat until sugar and peanut butter have dissolved. Cool marinade and reserve ¼ of the sauce. Add green onions and chicken thighs to marinade and soak overnight. Grill or broil chicken until cooked through. Baste with reserved sauce after chicken is cooked.

Teriyaki Sauce
Makes 1 quart

2 cups shoyu
2 cups sugar
¼ cup mirin
6 stalks green onion, cut into 1-inch pieces
4 (¼-inch) slices ginger, crushed
4 cloves garlic, crushed

Combine shoyu, sugar, mirin, green onion, ginger, and garlic in a bowl. Mix well until all the sugar dissolves. Store in the refrigerator.

Nori Chicken Burgers

Serves 3

1 pound ground chicken
1 egg
½ cup panko
¼ cup green onions, thinly sliced
1½ tablespoons furikake
½ teaspoon salt
¼ teaspoon pepper
Strips of nori
Oil for frying

Combine chicken, egg, panko, green onions, furikake, salt, and pepper in a bowl. Make small chicken patties and place a strip of nori on each one. Heat a pan with a few tablespoons of oil and fry until browned and cooked through.

Chicken Tofu

Serves 4

1½ **pounds chicken thighs, cut into strips** *(you may use pork too)*
1½ **tablespoons oil**
1 **onion, cut into ¼-inch pieces**
2 **tablespoons sake**
½ **cup shoyu**
½ **cup sugar**
1 **thumb-sized thin slice of ginger**
1 **(20-ounce) block firm tofu, cut into 1½-inch cubes**
1 **cup green onions, cut into 1-inch pieces**

In a pot on medium heat sauté chicken in oil until half cooked. Then add onions and cook until onions are soft and translucent. Add in sake, shoyu, sugar, and ginger and cook for a minute. Then add in tofu and simmer for a few minutes until heated through. Add in green onions and stir carefully so that the tofu doesn't break apart. Cook for another minute and take off heat.

Clam Chowder

Serves 4

½ pound bacon, sliced ¼-inch thick
½ of a medium onion, diced into ¼-inch pieces
2 large stalks of celery, diced into ¼-inch pieces
3 cups of milk
1 (14.75-ounce) can cream corn
1 (10.75-ounce) can condensed cream of mushroom soup
2 potatoes, cut into ½-inch cubes
1 teaspoon salt
¼ teaspoon pepper
2 (6.5-ounce) cans chopped clams, drained

In a large pot, cook bacon on medium high until crisp. Add in onions and celery; sauté until soft. Add in milk, cream corn, mushroom soup, potatoes, salt, and pepper. Bring to a boil; lower heat to a simmer and cook for 20 minutes, or until the potatoes are cooked through and the chowder is thickened. Before serving, add in the clams and stir well.

Matcha Green Tea Salmon
on Soba with a Sesame Miso Vinaigrette
Serves 4

1 pound dry soba
4 (6-ounce) fillets salmon
2 tablespoon olive oil
Pepper to taste
Sesame Miso Vinaigrette *(recipe follows)*
Matcha Tea Salt *(recipe follows)*
Green onions and toasted sesame seeds for garnish

Cook the soba in boiling water. Drain and rinse with cold water to prevent from sticking. Drizzle a little oil on the fillets and season lightly with pepper. Cook on a grill pan or in a frying pan with oil on medium high heat, until salmon is almost nicely seared on the outside and almost cooked through. The salmon will continue to cook even after taking off the heat, so do not over-cook.

To serve, dress soba sparingly with the vinaigrette. Sprinkle salmon liberally with the Matcha Tea Salt and place on soba. Garnish with green onions and toasted sesame seeds.

Matcha Tea Salt

1 tablespoon kosher salt
1 tablespoon matcha powder *(Matcha powder is highly recommended but you may use other green tea powders if matcha is unavailable)*

Combine the tea and salt; mix well.

Sesame Miso Vinaigrette

3 ounces Japanese seasoned rice vinegar
2 tablespoons sesame oil
2 tablespoons shoyu
2 tablespoons sugar
1 tablespoon toasted sesame seeds
1 tablespoon white miso
2 tablespoons vegetable oil
¼ teaspoon pepper

Combine all ingredients in a blender; mix well.

Garlic Butter Shrimp
and Mushrooms
Serves 2

2 teaspoons extra virgin olive oil
3 tablespoons Garlic Butter *(see page 121)*
8 ounces shrimp, shelled and deveined
4 ounces mushrooms, sliced ¼-inch thick
¼ teaspoon salt
⅛ teaspoon pepper
2 teaspoon sake
1 teaspoon parsley, chopped
Lemon wedges

In a non-stick frypan, heat oil and garlic butter on medium high heat. Add in shrimp, mushrooms, salt, pepper, and sake. Cook for a few minutes until shrimp is just done. Remove from heat, stir in chopped parsley, and serve with lemon.

Fried Shrimp

Serves 3

1 pound cleaned large shrimp with tails on
Salt and pepper to season
½ cup flour
2 eggs, beaten
2 cups panko *(Japanese bread crumbs)*

Dry shrimp on paper towels and lightly season with salt and pepper. Except for the tail, lightly dust shrimp in flour, then in egg wash, then in panko. Repeat the process until all shrimp are done. Deep-fry until golden and cooked through.

Shrimp Karaage
Serves 4

¼ cup shoyu
2 cloves garlic crushed
½ teaspoon salt
¼ teaspoon pepper
1 teaspoon sugar
2 tablespoon mirin
1½ pounds large shrimp, shelled and deviened
1 cup cornstarch
Oil for frying
Lemon wedges

Combine the shoyu, garlic, salt, pepper, sugar, and mirin in a bowl. Toss shrimp in the marinade well and let sit for a half hour. Dredge in cornstarch making sure to shake off the excess well, fry in hot oil. Cook until golden. Serve with lemon wedges.

Sauteed Shrimp
with Sun-Dried Tomato and Parsley Butter
Serves 3

5 tablespoons Sun-Dried Tomato and Parsley Butter *(see page 122)*,
  divided
1 pound shrimp, shelled and deveined
½ teaspoon salt
¼ teaspoon pepper
2 teaspoons white wine
Lemon wedges for garnish

Heat 3 tablespoons of the Sun-Dried Tomato and Parsley Butter in a pan on medium-high heat. Add shrimp, and season with salt and pepper. When the shrimp is half-way cooked, add in white wine and saute until shrimp is just cooked. Remove from heat and stir in the rest of the butter until melted and well incorporated.

Furikake Imitation Crab Noodles

Serves 6 as a side

½ pound thin spaghetti or angel hair pasta
3 fluid ounces oriental dressing
2 tablespoons furikake
½ pound imitation crab meat, shredded
½ large Japanese cucumber, cut in half lengthwise and thinly sliced crosswise
Sliced green onions for garnish

Cook pasta until done, cool under cold water, and drain well. Toss noodles with oriental dressing, furikake, imitation crab, and cucumber. Garnish with sliced green onions.

Grandma Geri's Nishime

Serves 6

1 ounce package nishime kombu
¾ cup shoyu
½ cup sugar
2 tablespoons sake
1 package (.35-ounce) dashi no moto
1½ pound boneless, skinless chicken thighs, cut into bite-sized pieces
1 (9-ounce) package konnyaku, cut into bite-sized pieces
2½ pounds of cut Nishime Vegetables *(see below)*

Wash and soak kombu in water for about 10 to 15 minutes. Tie kombu into knots and cut in between the knots. In a large saucepan on medium-high heat, combine the shoyu, sugar, sake, dashi no moto, kombu, and chicken. Cook until chicken is halfway cooked; add in the konnyaku and nishime vegetables. Cover pot, lower heat to medium, and cook for 25 to 30 minutes until vegetables are tender.

NISHIME VEGETABLES:

1 large carrot, cut into bite-sized pieces
1 small daikon, cut into bite-sized pieces
1 gobo, cut into bite-sized pieces
1 can bamboo shoots, sliced
1 small hasu, sliced
¾ lb araimo, cut into bite-sized pieces
8 shiitake mushrooms (fresh or reconstituted), cut in half

Sesame Eggplant

Serves 4 as a side

Oil for frying
½ cup Teriyaki Sauce *(see recipe on page 94 or use store-bought)*
2 teaspoon sesame oil
1 teaspoon sesame seeds, toasted
1 pound eggplant, washed and dried well with a paper towel, and cut into ½-inch thick slices
¼ cup green onions, sliced

Heat oil on medium high heat. In the meantime mix together in a large bowl, teriyaki sauce, sesame oil, and sesame seeds. Then fry eggplant for a few minutes until lightly browned and just cooked through, but not mushy. Remove eggplant from oil and put into sauce and toss until well coated. Garnish with green onions.

Chinese Roast Pork Salad
with Sesame Vinaigrette
Serves 4 to 6

1 large head romaine lettuce, sliced ¼-inch
1 small red bell pepper, thinly sliced
1 small carrot, julienned
1 large stalk celery, thinly sliced
1 small Japanese cucumber, cut in half and thinly sliced
1 small bunch cilantro, chopped *(optional)*
¾ cup green onions, sliced
½ pound roast pork, sliced
1 cup fried crispy noodles or wonton strips
Sesame Vinaigrette *(recipe follows)*

Toss together the lettuce, red bell peppers, carrots, celery, cucumber, cilantro, and green onions together in a bowl. Top with sliced roast pork and crispy noodles. To serve, dress lightly with sesame vinaigrette.

Sesame Vinaigrette

½ cup vegetable oil
3 tablespoons Japanese
   seasoned rice vinegar
1 tablespoon shoyu
⅛ cup sesame oil
¼ teaspoon pepper
½ teaspoon salt
1 teaspoon sugar
3 tablespoons plum sauce
1 teaspoon toasted
   sesame seeds

Put all ingredients into a jar and shake until well combined. Always shake well before dressing the salad.

Stir-Fry

Serves 2

Oil
    5 ounces protein
    4 cups mixed stir-fry vegetables
    ¼ cup stir-fry sauce
    (see recipes on the next page)
    1 tablespoon water

In a non-stick wok or large frying pan, heat oil on medium high to high heat. Add protein (except if using tofu, add in last with sauce) and cook until just cooked through. Add in vegetables and cook for a minute. Then add in sauce and water then cook for another minute. Do not overcook; vegetables should still be crisp.

PROTEIN SUGGESTIONS:

* Beef, pork, or chicken, thinly sliced
* Shrimp, shelled and deveined
* Scallops
* Firm tofu, drained well and cut into bite-sized pieces
* Fish, cut into bite-sized pieces

SUGGESTIONS FOR STIR-FRY VEGETABLE MIX:

* Chinese peas
* Mushrooms halves (if bigger, quarter)
* Carrots, julienned into ⅛-inch pieces
* Celery, sliced into ¼-inch pieces
* Onions, sliced into ¼-inch pieces
* Cabbage (won bok or head), cut into 1½-inch pieces
* Bell peppers, sliced ¼-inch
* Broccoli, 1-inch florets
* Bean sprouts
* Asparagus, cut into 1½-inch pieces
* String beans, cut into 1½-inch pieces

Stir-Fry Sauces

Hoisin Sauce
Makes about ¾ cup

½ cup shoyu
1 tablespoon hoisin
¼ cup sugar
1 clove garlic minced
1 tablespoon dry sherry
1 teaspoon sesame oil
¼ teaspoon pepper
1½ tablespoons cornstarch

Combine all ingredients and mix well.
Mix well again before using for stir-fry.

Chinese Black Bean Sauce
Makes about ¾ cup

½ cup shoyu
¼ cup sugar
2 cloves garlic, minced
1 tablespoon dry sherry
½ teaspoon ginger, grated
2 tablespoon oyster sauce
¼ teaspoon pepper
1 tablespoon Chinese
   black beans, rinsed and
   chopped
1½ tablespoons cornstarch

Combine all ingredients and mix well.
Mix well again before using for stir-fry.

Macaroni Salad

Serves 6 as a side

6 ounces (uncooked weight) elbow macaroni
3 ounces imitation crab, shredded
2 teaspoons grated carrots, squeezed of excess liquid
1 cup mayonnaise
1 teaspoon minced celery
1 teaspoon minced onion
½ teaspoon salt
¼ teaspoon pepper
¼ teaspoon sugar
⅛ teaspoon hondashi *(Japanese bonito fish soup base)*

Cook macaroni until soft, drain well, and cool completely. In a large bowl combine macaroni with imitation crab, carrots, mayonnaise, celery, onion, salt, pepper, sugar, and hondashi. Mix well and refrigerate for 4 hours. Before serving, mix well and add more mayonnaise if needed.

Pan-Seared Buttered Kabocha
Serves 4

1 pound kabocha, sliced into ¼-inch by 3-inch slices
¼ teaspoon salt
1 tablespoon brown sugar
2 tablespoons oil
2 to 3 tablespoons butter

In a large bowl, toss the sliced kabocha with the salt, brown sugar, and oil. Let sit for about 5 minutes. Heat a non-stick pan on medium to medium-high heat; add a tablespoon of butter for each batch of kabocha that you cook. Pan-fry the slices until cooked through, about a minute on each side

Cold Udon
Serves 4

1 pound dried udon noodles, cooked and then cooled under cold water
¼ cup green onions, thinly sliced
¼ cup Aji Momi nori
1 cup store-bought udon sauce or somen sauce

Place cold udon onto a plate or bowl. Garnish with green onions and nori. Serve with sauce on the side.

Chap Chae

Serves 4

4 ounces bean thread
6 dried shiitake mushrooms
1 egg, beaten
3 tablespoons shoyu
2 tablespoons sugar
1 tablespoon sesame oil
2 teaspoons mirin
2 teaspoons toasted sesame seeds
2 teaspoons salt
1 teaspoon pepper
1 tablespoon oil
1 small carrot,
    julienned
½ medium-sized
    onion, thinly
    sliced
2 cloves garlic,
    minced
¼ cup green onions,
    sliced

In a pot with boiling water cook bean thread for about 4 to 5 minutes until cooked. Drain and reserve. Soak dried shiitake mushrooms in hot water until reconstituted. Drain mushrooms, thinly slice, and reserve. Spray a small pan with nonstick spray and cook beaten egg on medium-low heat. Do not stir. Flip omelet when it sets, remove from heat, then thinly slice and reserve. Combine shoyu, sugar, sesame oil, mirin, sesame seeds, salt, and pepper in a large bowl. Then in a small pan add oil and sauté carrots, onion, garlic, and shiitake mushrooms for about 2 minutes. Add vegetables and bean thread to the large bowl with the sauce and mix well. Garnish with egg and green onions.

Sun-Dried Tomato Hummus
Serves 6

1 can garbanzo beans, drained
2 cloves garlic
¾ cup sun-dried tomatoes, drained
juice of ½ of a lemon
½ teaspoon salt
¼ teaspoon pepper
¾ cup water
½ cup extra virgin olive oil
1 tablespoon chopped parsley

Combine all ingredients except parsley in a food processor and puree until the hummus is smooth. Then add parsley and pulse until combined. Serve with pita, breadsticks, vegetables, or in a sandwich.

Fried Furikake Tofu

Serves 4

12 ounces firm or extra firm tofu, well
   drained and patted dry with
   paper towels
Salt for seasoning
2 eggs beaten mixed with
   1 heaping teaspoon of
   furikake
1 cup flour mixed with 2
   teaspoons furikake
Oil for frying
Dipping sauce *(recipe
   follows)*

Cut tofu in half, then into
½-inch slices. Season with
salt. Dredge in flour mixture,
shake off excess flour, and
dredge in egg mixture. Deep-fry
in hot oil until the outside is golden.
Serve with dipping sauce.

Dipping Sauce

¼ cup shoyu
¼ cup seasoned rice vinegar
1 teaspoon sesame oil
2 tablespoons thinly sliced green onions
1 teaspoon toasted sesame seeds
2 teaspoons sugar
1 clove garlic crushed

Combine all ingredients and mix well.

Soba and Edamame
with Citrus Shoyu Dressing
Serves 3

12.7 ounce package dry soba, cooked
1½ cup edamame, shelled and cooked
½ cup green onions, thinly sliced
Citrus Shoyu Dressing (recipe follows)

Toss cooked soba and edamame with dressing to taste, and top with green onions.

Citrus Shoyu Dressing

¼ cup shoyu
1 tablespoon honey
1 tablespoon sugar
⅛ cup freshly squeezed orange juice
⅛ cup Japanese seasoned rice vinegar
¼ cup vegetable oil
½ teaspoon salt
½ teaspoon Dijon mustard
⅛ teaspoon pepper

Combine all ingredients in a jar and shake well to combine.

Tamago

Serves 4 as a side

4 eggs
1 tablespoon sugar
1 teaspoon mirin
1 tablespoon water
½ teaspoon salt
Non-stick pan spray

Beat together all ingredients except non-stick pan spray. Heat a tamago egg pan (or a six inch non-stick fry pan) over medium low heat and spray with non-stick pan spray. Pour about ¼ cup of egg mixture into the pan and let cook until almost set; do not stir. From one end of the pan roll one side of the egg over about 1 inch and continue to roll egg over until the end. Spray pan again and pour in another ¼ cup of egg mixture. Repeat the process until all of the egg is used. Let cool slightly before cutting into slices.

VARIATIONS:

* To make **SPAM™ Tamago**, add 3 tablespoon chopped SPAM® to egg mixture.

* To make **Bacon Tamago**, add 2 to 3 tablespoons crisp crumbled bacon to egg mixture.

* To make **Green Onion Tamago**, add 2 tablespoons thinly-sliced green onions to egg mixture.

* To make **Char Siu Tamago**, add 2 tablespoons minced char siu to egg mixture.

* To make **Furikake Tamago**, add 1 tablespoon furikake to egg mixture.

* To make **Fish Cake Tamago**, add 2 tablespoons minced fish cake to egg mixture.

Mini Manapua
Makes 50

5 (7.5-ounce) cans buttermilk biscuit dough
Manapua filling *(see recipes that follow)*
1 egg beaten
Red food coloring and a clean small rubber stamp *(optional)*

Pre-heat oven to 400 degrees. Prepare a cookie sheet with parchment paper or silpat. Dust your workspace and hands with flour to prevent dough from sticking. There are 10 biscuits per container. Flatten a biscuit into a circle and place a heaping teaspoon of filling on the biscuit and pull sides together and crimp to form a ball. Place crimped side down on the pan. Right before baking, lightly brush top with egg wash and let dry for a minute. Put a drop of red food coloring on a plate, dip stamp in it and tapping off the excess, stamp the top of manapua. Bake for 12 minutes or until tops are golden brown.

Char Siu Filling

2 teaspoons vegetable oil
¾ pound char siu, diced ¼-inch thick
2 teaspoons shoyu
1½ tablespoon oyster sauce
1 tablespoon sugar
1 cup low sodium chicken broth
1¼ tablespoons cornstarch mixed with 1¼ tablespoons of water
3 tablespoons green onion, thinly sliced

Heat oil and sauté char siu until heated. Meanwhile, combine shoyu, oyster sauce, sugar, chicken broth, and cornstarch in a bowl and mix well. When char siu is heated, add the liquid mixture and cook until liquid reduced and thickened. Remove from heat and stir in green onions. Cool completely before assembling the manapua.

Garlic Chicken Filling

2 teaspoons vegetable oil
1¼ pound chicken thighs, diced
2 cloves garlic, minced
½ teaspoon salt
¼ teaspoon pepper
2 teaspoons shoyu
1½ tablespoon oyster sauce
1 tablespoon sugar
1 cup low-sodium chicken broth
1¼ tablespoons cornstarch mixed with 1¼ tablespoons of water
3 tablespoons green onion, thinly sliced

Heat oil and sauté chicken, garlic, salt, and pepper until cooked. Meanwhile, combine the shoyu, oyster sauce, sugar, chicken broth, and cornstarch mixture in a bowl and mix well. Add the sauce to chicken and cook until liquid is reduced and thickened. Remove from heat and stir in green onions. Cool completely before assembling the manapua.

Chikuwa Hotdogs

Serves 4 as a side

2 hotdogs
1 chikuwa *(tubular-shaped Japanese steamed fish cake)*

Either pan-fry or boil hotdog to cook. Set cooked hotdog aside to cool. Cut chikuwa into 2 pieces that are as long as the hotdog. Stuff cooled hotdogs into chikuwa and slice to serve.

Garlic Butter
Makes about 1 pound

1 pound salted butter, softened at room temperature
2 tablespoons extra virgin olive oil
¼ cup garlic, minced
1 teaspoon salt
½ teaspoon pepper
1 tablespoon parsley, minced

Using an electric hand mixer, whip butter on high for about 2 minutes. Then in a food processor, mince the garlic, olive oil, salt, and pepper together. Add the garlic mixture to the butter and whip together until well incorporated, about 1 minute. Add in parsley and mix again until evenly distributed.

GARLIC BREAD:

To make garlic bread, take a piece of bread or baguette and brush with melted garlic butter. Sprinkle with parmesan cheese, if desired, and toast in toaster oven or under a broiler until golden.

Sun-Dried Tomato
and Parsley Butter
Makes about 1 pound

1 pound salted butter, softened at room temperature
2 ounces sun-dried tomatos, drained
1 clove garlic
2 tablespoons olive oil
¼ teaspoon pepper
½ teaspoon salt
1 tablespoon parsley, minced

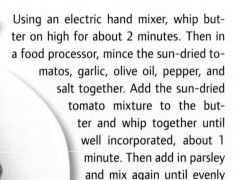

Using an electric hand mixer, whip butter on high for about 2 minutes. Then in a food processor, mince the sun-dried tomatos, garlic, olive oil, pepper, and salt together. Add the sun-dried tomato mixture to the butter and whip together until well incorporated, about 1 minute. Then add in parsley and mix again until evenly distributed.

SUN-DRIED TOMATO AND PARSLEY BUTTER BREAD:

To make sun-dried tomato and parsley butter bread, take a piece of bread or baguette and brush with melted Sun-Dried Tomato and Parsley Butter. Sprinkle with parmesan cheese, if desired, and toast in toaster oven or under a broiler until golden.

Guava Butter
Makes about 3 pounds

Guava Sauce

5 cups ripe guavas
½ cup water
2½ cups sugar
Juice of 1 lime

Trim off any blemishes and stems from guava. Add all ingredients in a saucepan. Bring to a boil, then lower heat and simmer for 20 minutes. Cool, then in batches, puree in a blender. Strain all the seeds out of the sauce.

Guava Butter

1 pound unsalted butter, softened
1 pound salted butter, softened
2 cups Guava Sauce *(recipe above)***

In a large mixing bowl, using an electric hand mixer, whip salted and unsalted butter for about 2 to 3 minutes until light and fluffy. Then add guava sauce in two batches to the butter and mix until well combined.

*As a short cut, you can also substitute your favorite preserves or jam to make a different kind of butter.

Glossary

Aji Momi Nori: Seasoned Japanese seaweed

Araimo: Japanese starchy taro-like potato

Char Siu: Sweet Chinese barbequed roast pork

Chinese Black Beans: Fermented black beans used in Chinese cooking

Chikuwa: Tubular-shaped Japanese steamed fish cake

Dashi no moto: Japanese powdered soup stock

Edamame: Soybeans

Furikake: Japanese dried rice seasoning

Gobo: Also known as burdock root. Long slender root used in dishes like nishime or kinpira gobo.

Hasu: Also known as lotus root, a white vegetable that is crisp in texture

Hoisin Sauce: Chinese barbeque dipping sauce

Kabocha: Japanese winter squash, but commonly referred to as Japanese pumpkin

Katsuobushi: Dried shaved bonito flakes

Kamaboko: Japanese steamed fish cake

Kombu: Dried Japanese kelp

Konnyaku: Made from Japanese mountain yams, it is sold in block form which is jelly like in consistency

Manapua: In Hawai'i, it is the pidgin term for Chinese steamed or baked buns filled with pork. Also can be found filled with other fillings.

Matcha Powder: Type of green tea in powder form

Mirin: Japanese sweet rice wine

Musubi: Japanese rice ball

Nishime: A Japanese dish made of a mix of vegetables, and sometimes a protein, simmered in a sweet shoyu broth.

Nori: Dried sheets of seaweed

Shoyu: Japanese term for soy sauce

Soba: Japanese buckwheat noodles

Somen: Thin white Japanese wheat-flour noodles

Tamago: Japanese term for eggs

Udon: Japanese thick wheat-flour noodle

Wakame: Mild flavored Japanese seaweed, found usually in dried form

Bento Index

Recipe Index

About the Author

Susan was born and raised in Hilo, Hawai'i and moved to Honolulu where she continues to reside. She and her husband Mark have two children, Paige and Sean Patric.

Following her move to Honolulu, Susan worked in the food industry for many years. Her love for cooking and feeding people eventually led her to a career as a sous-chef at two well-known local restaurants, Palomino Euro-Bistro and Kincaid's as well as a co-owner of a catering company. Susan's career in the food industry came to a halt in 2002 when she gave birth to Paige and decided to devote herself full-time as a wife and mother. In 2008, Susan started the blog *Hawai'i's Bento Box Cookbook, Bentos and More for Kids.*

Susan Yuen
Email: syuen14@gmail.com
http://susanyuen.wordpress.com/